A Quiet, Happy Place

ISBN: 978-0-692-94143-0

for Charlotte and Samantha
with special love

A labyrinth is a quiet, happy place.

A labyrinth is not a maze . . .

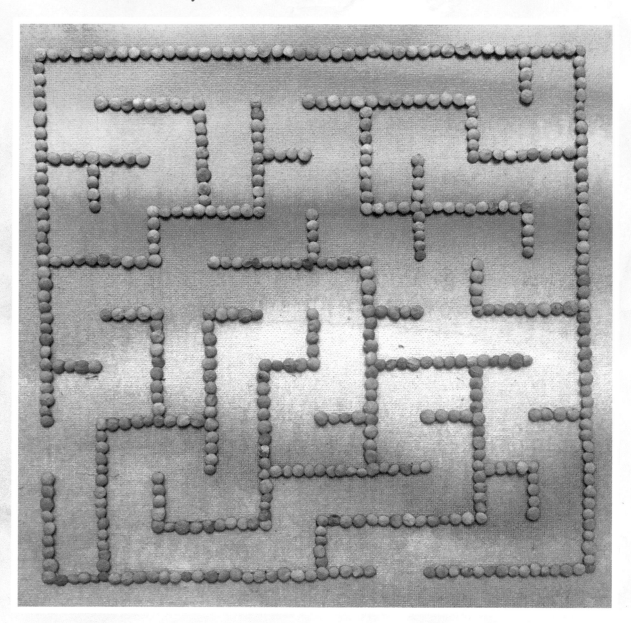

where you can make mistakes, wrong turns, get lost.

When you step into a labyrinth, you relax.

Breathe.

You can't mess up!

Put one foot in front of the other.

Set your own pace.

Enjoy the twists and turns!

Labyrinths come in many different shapes,

sizes, and designs.

Some are very small,

while others are very large.

Some are very simple,

while others are very intricate.

But they all have just one path . . .

to the center and back out again.

You can find labyrinths in unexpected places . . .

Urban Labyrinth - 5Pointz Aerosal Art Center, Queens, NY.

on ancient coins,

woven in baskets,

in flower gardens,

and floor tiles,

in the woods,

by the sea,

and even in the snow!

Labyrinths can be made of almost anything . . .

from Fruit Loops

to flower petals,

Lincoln Logs

to linguini.

Follow the Labyrinth Seed Pattern

and you can make one, too!

When you encounter a labyrinth, you know . . .

it's time to take time out ~ for time in.

Imagine.

Dream.

A labyrinth is a quiet, happy place

to listen to your heart.

More About the Labyrinth

What is a Labyrinth?

A labyrinth is both a rich symbol and a powerful tool. Part of its magic and allure is that nobody knows the origins of the labyrinth, nor are there any clues as to how labyrinths came to flourish in cultures widely separated by time and space. Labyrinths are known to have existed for more than 3,500 years. They have been found in North and South America, Africa, Asia, and across Europe from the Mediterranean to Scandinavia. Unlike a maze, a labyrinth presents no tricks, choices, challenges or dead-ends. A meandering, single or "unicursal" path leads from the entrance to the center and back. Labyrinths are sacred spaces, works of art, places to celebrate and play, and places for introspection and healing.

Why walk a Labyrinth?

Today, labyrinths are used primarily for purposes of meditation, reflection and centering. Walking the labyrinth is a right-brain activity (creative, intuitive, imaginative) and can induce or enhance a contemplative state of mind and elicit a "relaxation response." Gael D. Hancock, author of *108 Ways to Use Labyrinths in Schools*, has found that labyrinths engage children's natural creativity, help children find answers to inner questions, help children calm and focus, and provide a safe place for recognizing and sharing feelings. The demonstrated health benefits of walking a labyrinth have led hundreds of hospitals, healthcare facilities, retreat centers, and spas, as well as schools, municipalities, and individuals to install labyrinths in recent years.

Find a labyrinth near you using the World-Wide Labyrinth Locator (labyrinthlocator.com).

About the Author

Melinda Cropsey is the founder of Heart's Path, LLC, and the author of the Heart's Path Curriculum (a social-emotional curriculum designed for children between the ages of 3 and 7). She is also a textile designer and labyrinth enthusiast. She conducts heart-centering labyrinth workshops for children of all ages. With the help of her husband and three sons, she built this labyrinth at her home in Longmeadow, MA.

Acknowledgements

I am so grateful to all of the children, teachers, and families with whom I have had the pleasure of sharing my labyrinth enthusiasm! I am especially grateful to the children I have worked with in developing the Heart's Path Curriculum. They have taught me so much more than I could possibly have taught them about the workings of the heart and our innate capacity for empathy, compassion, and connection.

I also want to thank the global community of labyrinth lovers who have generously agreed to allow me to include their photos in *A Quiet, Happy Place*.

Graphics and layout by Giada Rose